J
550
SI

Sipiera, Paul P.

I can be a
geologist

$13.27

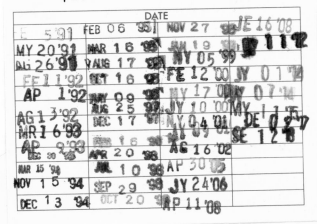

DATE			
FE 5'91	FEB 06 '91	NOV 27 '98	JE 16 '08
MY 20'91	MAR 16 '93	JA 19 '99	P 11'12
AU 26'91	AUG 17 '93	MY 05 '99	
FE 11'92	OCT 16 '93	FE 12 '00	JY 01'14
AP 1'92	MY 09 '95	MY 17 '00	MY 07'14
AG 13'92	AG 25 '97	JY 10 '00	MY 1 1 15
MR 16'93	DEC 17 '97	MY 04 '01	DE 0 3'17
AP 9'93	FE 16 '98	JL 09 '01	SE 12'18
DEC 30 '93	APR 20 '98	AG 16 '02	
MAR 15 '94	JL 10 '98	AP 30 '05	
NOV 15 '94	SEP 29 '98	JY 24 '06	
DEC 13 '94	OCT 20 '98	AP 11 '08	

© THE BAKER & TAYLOR CO.

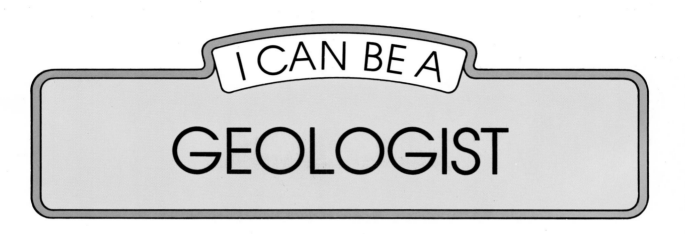

I CAN BE A

GEOLOGIST

By Paul P. Sipiera

Prepared under the direction of Robert Hillerich, Ph.D.

CHILDRENS PRESS ®
CHICAGO

Library of Congress Cataloging-in-Publication Data
Sipiera, Paul P.
  I can be a geologist.

  (I can be)
  Summary: Briefly describes a variety of jobs and
topics of study in the field of geology and highlights
the necessary education and training.
  1. Geology—Vocational guidance—Juvenile literature.
[1. Geology—Vocational guidance. 2. Vocational
guidance. 3. Occupations] I. Title. II. Series.
QE34.S57   1986   550'.23   86-9598
ISBN 0-516-01897-3

PICTURE DICTIONARY

dinosaur

volcano

fossil

glacier

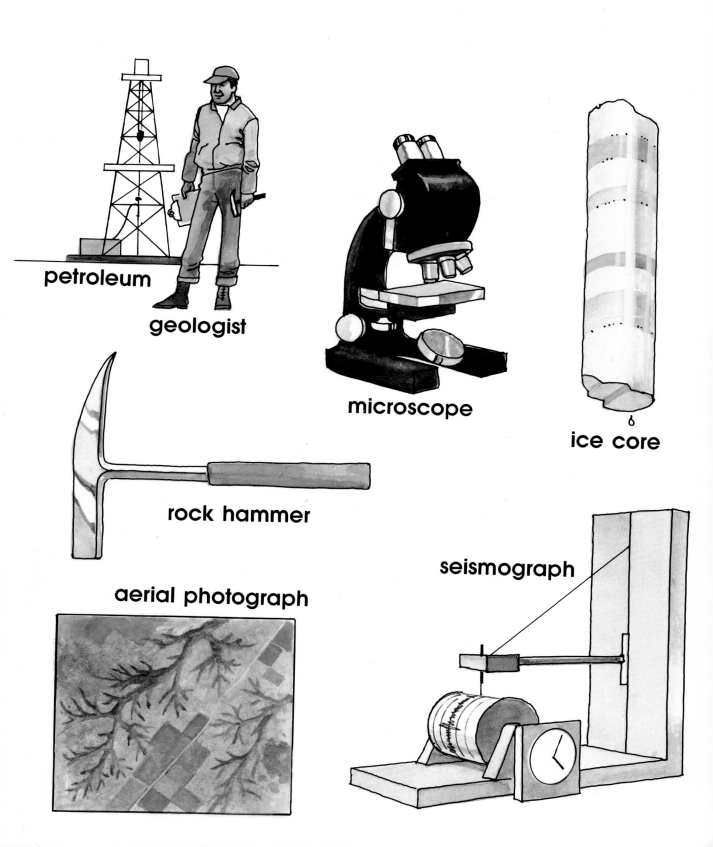

petroleum

geologist

microscope

ice core

rock hammer

aerial photograph

seismograph

Above: Scientists digging for dinosaur bones in Utah
Below: Bones discovered in Dinosaur National Monument, an area
in Utah and Colorado where dinosaurs once lived

dinosaur

Where do rocks come from? What did a dinosaur look like? Why does a volcano erupt? Questions like these are answered by geologists.

geologist

Geologists study the earth and the materials it is made of. There are many different kinds of geologists. Some search for oil and precious metals. Others look for

volcano

A fossilized fish

fossil

water within the earth's surface.

Geologists called paleontologists study fossils. Fossils are plant and animal parts or prints left in stone. They

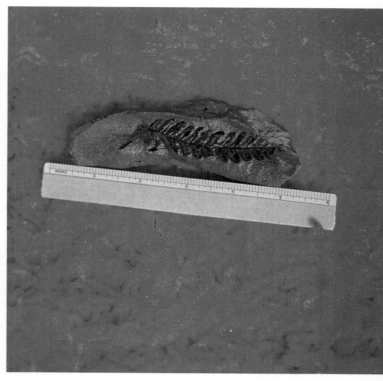

Left: Fossil shells in limestone.   Right: This fossil fern is 350 million years old.

show us what life was
like millions of years
ago.

Many geologists work
for oil companies and
search for petroleum.
Petroleum is used to

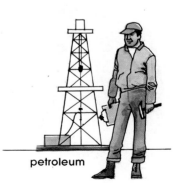

petroleum

make gasoline for our cars. It also heats our homes. Many fertilizers and medicines are also made from petroleum.

Searching for petroleum may take geologists to faraway lands. It is not easy to find. Often geologists find petroleum offshore beneath the ocean floor.

Geologist recording information on materials under the earth's surface

Geologists also find underground water for people to drink. Some geologists study rivers to prevent floods. Others try to prevent water pollution. It is very important to keep our water pure.

Above: Geologist working on a map showing the underground composition of an area. Below: A diagram showing a cross-section of the earth

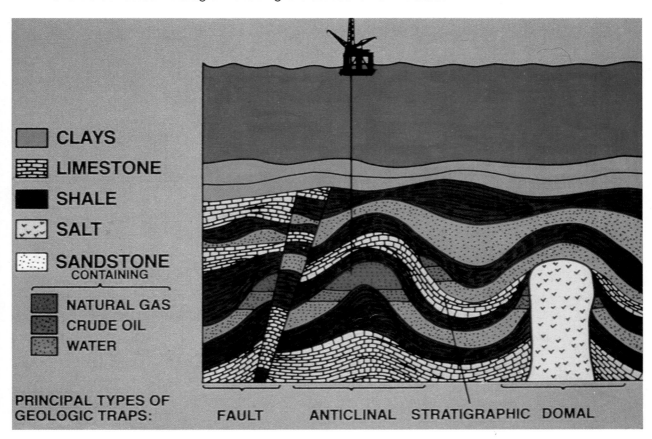

CLAYS

LIMESTONE

SHALE

SALT

SANDSTONE
CONTAINING

NATURAL GAS

CRUDE OIL

WATER

PRINCIPAL TYPES OF
GEOLOGIC TRAPS:

FAULT   ANTICLINAL   STRATIGRAPHIC   DOMAL

Studying the movement of glaciers in an Alaska icefield

ice core

glacier

Geologists may also study glaciers—huge blocks of ice as big as mountains. They drill out long, tubelike sections from the glacier, called ice cores. The ice core

Geologists' equipment: a rock hammer (left) and a Brunton compass (right)

shows what the earth's climate was like thousands of years ago.

A geologist uses many tools to learn about the earth. A rock hammer is used to chip or break rocks. A Brunton compass is used in making maps

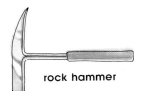

rock hammer

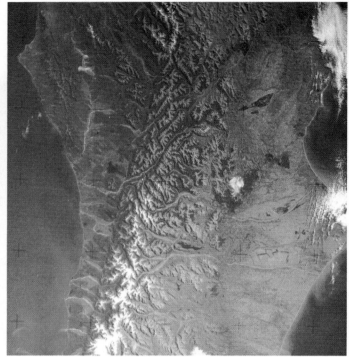

Above: Utah and Colorado, taken from the *Landsat* satellite
Right: Part of New Zealand, taken from *Skylab 4*

aerial photograph

of rock formations. Aerial photographs, which are taken from the sky, help geologists better understand what they are mapping.

Photographs taken from space can show

14

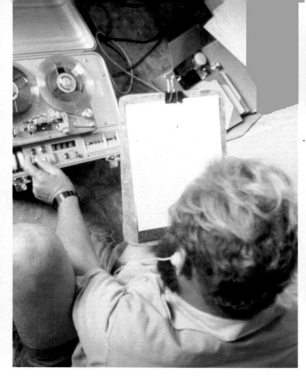

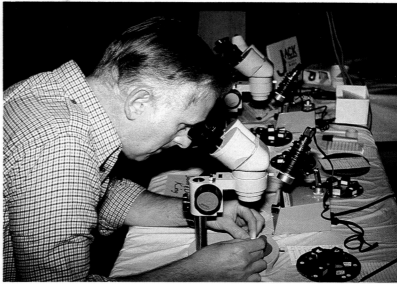

Left: Recording earth tremors
Above: Examining a mineral under a microscope

an entire chain of mountains in one photograph. They are used in exploring for minerals and petroleum.

Geologists also use microscopes to study rocks. They use seismographs to

microscope

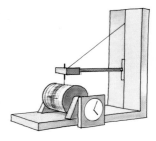

seismograph

Left: Seismograph.   Right: A geologist studying the information gathered by a seismograph

measure earthquakes
and to study rocks far
below the earth's
surface.

Everything we
depend on for our lives
comes from the earth's
surface. The earth is
covered by oceans

A basalt cliff

and areas of land
called continents.
Under the oceans is a
rock called basalt. It is
the most common rock
on earth. The continents
are made of many
different rocks.

Rocks are made of

Left: This highway was cut through layers of limestone. Right: Copper (top) and gold (bottom)

minerals. Most of the minerals we use come from the continents. We use minerals to make cars and to construct buildings. Minerals supply us with the iron that is made into steel. Cement is made from a

Mining copper in Montana (left) and gold in South Africa (right)

rock called limestone.

Gold and copper are valuable minerals. We use copper for electrical wires and water pipes. Gold is used in coins and jewelry. A diamond is another precious mineral.

Geologists can tell us much about the world we live on. They have shown us what the earth is like on the inside. Earthquakes and volcanoes begin deep within the earth. They can be very destructive. Geologists hope to learn how to predict earthquakes. This will save many people's lives and property.

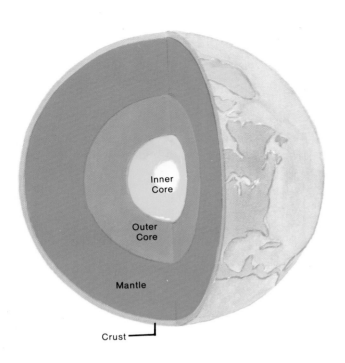

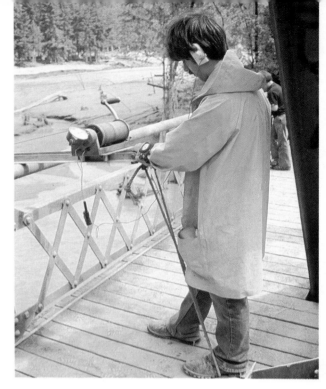

Upper right: Geologist measuring river sediment after Mount Saint Helens Volcano erupted in the state of Washington. Below: Glowing lava erupts from Paricutin Volcano in Mexico.

Geologists have made many exciting discoveries. For example, they have found that all the continents may once have been joined together. Today they are moving apart. This is called continental drift.

Earth is a living planet. It is always changing. Given

Left: Geologists at an international seminar on oil and energy in Hawaii. Right: Surveying land in Colorado for a geological study

enough time, anything is possible. Large mountains are formed and then washed away. It takes millions of years for this to happen.

Left: Geologist cutting a soil sample
Right: A plain on the surface of Mars,
as photographed by a *Viking* space probe

Today geologists
have gone beyond the
earth. Geologists have
collected rocks on the
moon and have
learned about the soil
on Mars.

Scientist-astronaut Harrison Schmitt rakes up moon rocks with a lunar rake.

An artist's concept of a supply base on the moon, where lunar
soil might be processed as raw material for industry.

Some planets are like
the earth. Others, like
Jupiter, are very
different. Someday
geologists will help find
valuable minerals on
the moon that can be
used on earth.

What does it take to become a geologist? You must like to work outdoors. Geologists work in some very exciting places. Some go to Antarctica where it is cold all year around. Others may work all alone in the desert. Not all people may want to be a geologist.

Left: Student examining fossil rocks.   Right: Young
scientists cleaning rocks and minerals for a display

To be a geologist you
must study very hard.
Chemistry, mathematics,
and physics are very
important subjects to
learn. It takes many
years of study and hard
work.

Geologists' work may take them to faraway places. Left: On the
Juneau, Alaska, icefield.   Right: In the Canadian wilderness

But once you
become a geologist,
you may go to a place
where no one has ever
been before. Or make
a wonderful discovery
that will benefit many
people. It can be a
very exciting life!

29

WORDS YOU SHOULD KNOW

aerial photograph (EHR • ee • ul FOH • tuh • graf)—a picture of the earth taken from an airplane

basalt (BAY • salt)—a rock formed from lava that flows from a volcano

Brunton compass (BRUN • tun KOM • pus)—a special compass used by geologists to help them make maps of rock formations

continent (KAHN • tih • nent)—one of seven large areas of land on the earth, most of them separated from one another by the oceans

dinosaur (DY • nuh • sahr)—a giant reptile that lived on earth millions of years ago

earthquake (ERTH • kwayk)—a shaking or trembling of the earth caused by rock movements deep within the earth

fossil (FOSS • ul)—parts or prints of plants or animals that have been left in stone or have turned into stone

glacier (GLAY • sher)—a large mass of ice that flows out of high mountain valleys

ice core—a tube-shaped section of ice drawn out of a glacier to study its layers

limestone (LYM • stone)—a rock composed mostly of the remains of living things, such as shells or coral. It is often used to make building materials.

microscope (MY • kruh • skope)—an instrument that gives an enlarged view of very small objects

minerals (MIN • er • ulz)—basic components that rocks are made of

paleontologist (pay • lee • un • TOL • uh • jist)—a scientist who studies fossils to understand what life on earth was like millions of years ago

petroleum (puh • TROH • lee • um)—a dark, oily liquid that burns. It is used to make gasoline and other energy-producing substances.

seismograph (SIZE • moh • graf)—an instrument that measures vibrations within the earth, for instance, during an earthquake

volcano (vol • KAY • no)—a crack in the earth's crust from which steam and lava (melted rock) pour out. Over the years, the lava piles up and becomes a mountain.

INDEX

PHOTO CREDITS

ABOUT THE AUTHOR

Paul Sipiera is an Associate Professor of Physical Sciences at William Rainey Harper College in Palatine, Illinois, and a research associate in geology at the Field Museum of Natural History in Chicago. As a member of the National Science Foundation's Antarctic Research Program, he has studied geological features of the icy continent. Mr. Sipiera is technical advisor to Society Expedition's Project Space Voyage, the first venture into space for the general public. A teacher of astronomy and geology, his specialties are meteorites, moon rocks, and volcanoes. Mr. Sipiera gardens, grows vegetables, and plants maple trees at his home in Crystal Lake, Illinois.